LIST YOUR LIFE

Listing the Risks You Can Take
To Enhance Your Life

(Previously published as *Risk Your Self*)

**ILENE SEGALOVE AND
PAUL BOB VELICK**

**MJF BOOKS
NEW YORK**

Published by MJF Books
Fine Communications
Two Lincoln Square
60 West 66th Street
New York, NY 10023

List Your Life
LC Control Number 00-135985
ISBN 1-56731-438-4

Copyright © 2000 by Ilene Segalove and Paul BobVelick

This edition published by arrangement with Andrews McMeel Publishing.
This book was previously published under the title *Risk Your Self.*

Book Design by Lisa Martin

Manufactured in the United States of America on acid-free paper

MJF Books and the MJF colophon are trademarks of Fine Creative Media,
Inc.

10   9   8   7   6   5   4   3   2   1

*This journal is for all those who introduced me
to the early spirits of damp fields yet walked,
of fertile forests still asleep, of personal paths
very carefully carved. It is to the intoxicating
courage found when following the scent and soul
of the inspired unknown. . . . **I'll meet you there**.
To Goodman Herman Fred Stuart Harry,
Jon Henry David and Larry.*

—Paul Bob Velick

*This is a tribute to all of you who have shown,
by example, the amazing vigor and grace inherent
in the act and art of risk taking. I salute your
unabashed willingness to expose yourself (without
bowing to possible loss or infinite what-ifs) to the
elements, to each other, and most daring, to your-
selves. Thank you for leaping into what's possible
without needing to take a bow or raise a ruckus.
Hats off. And now a standing ovation!*

—Ilene Segalove

Contents

Introduction

(Note: This book was formerly published as *Risk Your Self*)

L ife is risk. Not just the obvious big stuff like sky-diving or bungee jumping, taking a spin on the space shuttle or dashing into a burning building to save a life. Everyday life is risky, but we're used to it. Only when we make a leap in our relationships or our careers do we stop and gasp, "Wow. This could be a risk (gulp)!" And then the self-doubt and endless inner chatter begins: "What if I fail? What if I embarrass myself? What if I come up short. . . ."

We are great naysayers. We tell ourselves, "Be realistic." We wallow in worry and we get stuck with what's at stake: "There's so much to lose!" In doing so we end up letting fear run the show. Caution has its place, of course. But in our struggle to make sense, we often strangle our very best—our zest, the oomph, the longing—that, when expressed, gives our lives its flavor, meaning, and purpose. Suddenly the joy of taking risks turns into a battle with reason. We avoid risk and we play it safe.

We call this living in our "comfort zone," but is it *really* comfortable? It often makes us numb to life and to each other. Periodically we may ask ourselves, "Is this it? Is this really *my* life?" Most of the time we avoid the question altogether because it is too troubling and requires that we change.

Percolating inside each one of us is a calling—a call to risk—to jump, dance, scream, invent, soar, act, to break loose! It comes from a deep impulse that challenges our status quo and asks us to grow. *Risk Your Self* encourages us to list the risks and rewards of making that leap. It inspires us to reach inside to embrace risk as part of our everyday living. The simple act of listing the pros and cons of personal change will uncover the infinite possibilities lurking inside your heart and mind. Risk risking yourself!

Risk Your Self gives you permission to figure out what you really want and launches you in the right direction. By exploring different levels of risk taking you'll learn to identify your own current personal risks. You will also cultivate your skills in taking risks and will map out the steps you need to venture ahead.

Risk Your Self gives you the tools and the vision to soar a little higher. It's a safe way to practice taking risks. Whatever the risk may be, you'll get a chance to try it out on paper first! *Risk Your Self* opens your eyes and your ears to living life to the fullest. You can reshape your career and improve your relationships, or rediscover what you love and what you may be neglecting. Consider this an invitation to ensure that your life reflects your personal best.

What Are Risks?

Risks are actions that put us on the line. They usually involve a lot of unknowns. Not knowing results. Not knowing all the "right" steps to reach a goal. Not knowing what's around the corner. Not knowing if things will turn out the way we hope. It means not being in control, and with lack of control comes all the feelings of fear and confusion as well as a good dose of excitement and exhilaration. You step out so far that you are convinced there is no going back—and you may be right.

For example, Lucy said leaving her first marriage was the biggest risk she had ever taken. She sought the advice of a few friends who tried to talk her out of it. Then, one day, she just left, without a plan as to what the next stage of her life would look like.

"It was like jumping off a cliff. I considered it a multiple risk. I risked being ostracized by everyone I knew (I wasn't). I risked falling into deep financial trouble

(I didn't). I risked never owning a house again (I did). But my deepest self was truly committed to this risk. I think if I hadn't left I would have risked even more: dying, at least metaphorically. I didn't! What I gained by taking the risk was a huge lesson. My life didn't end that day—it actually began with that risk."

Taking a risk is usually a private venture. Asking advice brings the obvious response: "Are you serious?" or worse, "Are you nuts?" or "Only a fool would take that kind of risk." Your logical mind may know full well this is a big risk, but another part of you screams to explore, to find out what you are really made of. Inside you know that only by taking certain risks can you test your limits and uncover some of your brightest truths. Here's another example.

Addison risked changing careers in midlife. "I had to face myself. I had to admit I was living like a robot. So I took out a huge student loan, put myself and my bank account on the line. Everyone told me it would be a financial disaster. I left a secure tenured position at forty-six years old. The risks were staggering but the risk of staying seemed more so. I am strapped financially, it is true. I wish I had thought this risk out a little bit better. It would have helped me prepare for what was up ahead. I've been haunted by a good deal of insecurity. I love what I am now doing. The risk was tough but totally worth it."

If you look back on your own life, you'll notice many of the most important turning points, the ones that made you who you are today, were the risks you dared to take. Many of those risks could have affected your life in an even more positive way if you had the tools to "work" them, to explore the pros and cons and to consider the best action steps. *Risk Your Self* gives you the chance to try out your risks before you take them. You can check out the risks of leaving a relationship without having to leave. You can start a new business without taking out a loan or leave for an exotic vacation without getting on an airplane. It's a little like target practice. You'll learn how to aim and fire first, without getting hurt. Guaranteed, you won't fall on your face. And then if you like what you see and what you feel—risk it! Consider some of the many big risks you have taken that have changed your life for the better.

List the most significant risks you've ever taken.
- Giving birth underwater to my daughter
- Marrying outside my race
- Getting a divorce
- Working overseas
- Locating and living with my "real" father after being adopted by someone else
- Joining a monastery and living in silence
- Being a medic in Vietnam
- Admitting I am gay
- Selling my house and leaving my family to travel in a van for two years
- Leaving the security of corporate life to pursue my own enterprise
- Traveling alone to the Far East

Reckless Risks

There are all kinds of risks, from driving on the freeway to getting involved with the "wrong" person. All decisions are risks to a certain degree. The more you know and the more experience you have—tempered with some common sense and faith—the more confident you may feel taking a risk. But no matter the preparation, some risks are just plain dangerous, crazy, or reckless. It really depends on the individual taking them. One person's big risk is another person's "no big deal." For example, losing twenty pounds for a very thin person is a dangerous risk; it could put their health in serious jeopardy. Losing twenty pounds for someone who has a heart condition and is overweight is simply a huge risk not to risk. Get it?

Of course, some risks are reckless for everyone. Most of us have taken risks that we knew weren't good for us but we did them anyway. We don't want to admit it, but we all share a long list in the reckless risk department: Smoking, taking drugs, driving under the influence, engaging in unprotected sex, quitting our jobs without having any money in the bank ... the list goes on. These are foolish gambles—based mostly on ignorance—with no possible gain at the end.

List the most reckless risks you've taken.
- Running a red light
- Snorting aerosol propellant
- Buying land in some obscure place over the phone
- Going to Hollywood to get famous
- Eating pork off a street cart in Mexico
- Driving drunk
- Hitchhiking
- Carrying an unregistered weapon in the car
- Traveling to Cambodia and not taking malaria medication
- Taking LSD
- Dying my hair green
- Jumping off a really high cliff into an icy river
- Falling in love with a psycho
- Buying stocks without doing any real research
- Gambling in Las Vegas when I hardly had any money
- Having a child at fifteen
- Marrying the first guy who asked me

Monique recalls a "senseless risk" that still haunts her. "The one big risk I took and lost was waiting for the time to be right to apologize to my mother. We had a rocky relationship and I was really hard on her. It was a real risk to even call her up to talk with her. I kept hedging my bets and telling myself I had time. I'll do it next week. The risk of being honest with her was daunting. One day she died rather suddenly. That was that. I lost. I wish I had had the courage to take the risk of telling her I loved her. Instead I risked believing time was on my side, when it wasn't."

Risk Your Self is dedicated to helping you practice and take solid, timely risks that promote your best in self-expression, creativity, and stretching your life possibilities. *Risk Your Self* encourages you to go out on a mental limb. It allows you to take a leap of faith, without leaping, or better yet, without falling. The power of practicing risk is profound. It is a way to savor the process and the possibilities without having to suffer the damage. It's a way to avoid taking more reckless risks.

The Risk Taking Muscle

Like any new venture, taking risks requires you to get in shape. The risk challenges in this book support the development of your "risk taking" muscle. Taking risks is similar to adding five more push-ups to your daily regime of ten. Moving through the risk challenges in *Risk Your Self* will arouse your nerve endings and stimulate your curiosity. You will become agile at responding to risks. Once you see the benefits, you will become a believer and take more risks in your daily life. It's an additive skill that will not only expand your imagination, but will improve your quality of life. Just flex this new behavioral muscle and see what happens.

You may never find taking risks a breeze. If it were, would they call it a "risk"? It's meant to be a real test, an opportunity to find out your true character. But by practicing, you'll tune in to the call, the adventure, the whistle, the desire, and when you are good and ready, you'll have the courage and stamina to show up and be counted in areas you never considered before. Risk taking is something to get good at. Why be flabby in the risk taking area? You'll miss out on too much.

How Does It Work?

Risk Your Self gives you the opportunity to consider all kinds of risks. It is divided into five main sections. Get warmed up with Everyday Risks—consider "Risk eating something different for breakfast." An easy risk such as substituting oatmeal for sweet rolls shouldn't be too much of a challenge. But try it; it could upset your whole day! Easy risks show us how deeply our habits are ingrained. They define who we are, even the seemingly banal toast-and-jelly kind of habits.

Now, if you want to practice risking something a little bigger, move into Real Risks. This section features hypothetical risks about money, family, and adventure, just to name a few. Try one on for size. Let's say you want to "Risk starting your own business." This is the place to give it a shot. List your worst fears, common excuses, and the pros and cons of taking the risk. Explore your dreams and then decide what you want to do.

If you are feeling brave, explore Risking the Truth. It's the ultimate risk. Consider "Risk telling the truth to your boss about . . ." And if you want to lighten up, check out Fantasy Risks. These are opportunities to take risks that drop you into the realm of escape and what-if's . . ." Then spend some quality time customizing your Personal Risk lists to delve into the current risks you face today. Evaluating all sides of a risk helps you let go of the trepidation you bring to taking risks. Risking is part courage, part faith. Why let fear skew your vision? Write it down and let it go.

The key to *Risk Your Self* is writing down your own truth, in your own words. When you fill in the blanks you'll uncover what you think and feel, what makes you tick. The many provocative risk scenarios will stimulate your heart and mind and get you into "thinking risk." Writing is a powerful process. It's an elegant way to reconnect with your deepest self. Without much effort the true story about your risks will show up on paper.

Of course there will always be excuses that pop up. We all make them because they give us an out. They keep our impulses in check. They are sometimes the wise voice of reason. But when it comes to risks, we *need* to let these go; they hold us back and keep us down.

List all the excuses you make for not risking.

- I don't have the time.
- I don't have the money.
- I don't really feel like it.
- I have too many responsibilities.
- I'm too tired, too afraid, too lazy.
- What will my friends say? What will my family say?
- What if I fail? What if I embarrass myself? There's too much at stake.
- What's the use?
- Isn't that being too self-indulgent? I don't deserve the possible rewards.

And on and on . . .

Remember, listing risks gives you the opportunity to try out all kinds of risks and to really connect with the feelings they generate and the possibilities or dangers they may provoke. You can list your excuses and continue the process; they don't need to stop you. As you write, you'll link up with your subconscious, the place inside our minds that really doesn't know the difference between fiction, flights of fantasy, and reality. You'll shift into another kind of thinking and sensing and you'll live the risks a little as you consider their impact and their repercussions in your life. It will free you up to muse and wonder, to think before you act, to express your fears in a safe environment, and to stretch and flex your risk taking muscle.

Over time you'll develop a new relationship with risks. You'll become more conversant with the part of you that wants to take a chance, that wants to change. You'll find yourself telling people how you really feel. You'll develop a stronger sense of what's right and what's wrong. You'll even resurrect your sense of spirit and adventure.

Risk Taking Anatomy

Let's say you are in a relationship and you don't know if you should stay or go. You know either choice is a risk. You locate the topic "Change" in the Real Risks chapter and choose "Risk leaving a relationship that isn't nurturing." Just the experience of sitting down to focus helps you feel more in tune with yourself. Your agitation level lessens. You see possibilities emerge and you'll have more choices than you thought. Each risk taking scenario gives you new insight. In time, you feel clearer and stronger about your resolve.

Consider the relationship you are thinking about leaving. Here's the scoop:

- You are living your ordinary life filled with lots of things to do and obligations to take care of.

- Every now and then you get an impulse to do something else. It's kind of a call to adventure. You consider a risk. (In this case, leaving a relationship.)

- You pick up *Risk Your Self* and turn to the appropriate chapter (in this case, Real Risks/Change).

- You make the typical excuses: "I'm afraid. What if I'm wrong? What will my friends think? I'm too old, too tired, too uninspired." You fill in the blanks. You've seen this list too many times before.

- And yet you still hear this calling. You say "Okay" and decide to give it a shot. In doing so you commit to crossing into working out the risk. First you "List the risks," all those thoughts of fear and loathing, and then dive into "List the worst scenario." Ah yes, time to really indulge.

- A few pieces of you are revealed. Gulp. You have moved from spectator and fearful thinker to actually playing the game. You have unleashed energy and vigor. Wow. Looking at the worst you suddenly feel hopeful. What's happening?

- Nothing can stop you now. "List the rewards" turns into a treasure chest of unearthed potential. Something tangible is showing up! Now you can move out into the world and actually do it, or stay put, safe on the page. Maybe you'll do it later. No rush.

- Now you are excited and a little bit confused. You realize there may be some sacrifices to make. You consider "List what you are willing to do" and notice a plan of action taking shape. Who's writing here? Who's so smart? Surprise. You *are* willing to do something. Change is in the air! Remember, it's almost impossible to fake these lists. You can't lie on paper—it's too obvious. You may feel like you are falling apart for a second; there goes life as you know it. Thank goodness! It wasn't working. As the fear and the possibilities clarify themselves right before your eyes you'll discover some real solid life-changing options . . . in your own words and not some authority's.

- Whether you decide to take action or not, you have illuminated your situation; a new perception and sense of self is in the making. No matter what the "real" or imagined steps you decide to take are, you will change and grow for the better.

Taking Risks Pushes Your Buttons

It is risky to risk. It requires change, and change is scary. That's why most people avoid it at all costs and prefer their predictable, "normal" lives. Change threatens your reality; it breaks your patterns. *Risk Your Self* lets you try on different risky challenges without having to actually live them. It gives you a chance to experience what it's like without actually stepping off the cliff. It teaches you that all risks aren't precursors of danger, chaos, and the complete dissolution of all that we love, all that we've worked so hard for. Different risks feed us in different ways. Some risk feeds our souls, others infuse our work with more joy or financial reward.

Let's say you choose "Risk not arguing for a change" in the Everyday Risks chapter. Your sister calls you up and she knows how to push your buttons. She starts to blame you for something and you become agitated. Your normal reaction is to fight back, and part of you loves it. Who else could you talk to in this way?

And then you remember today's risk, and you sneak a peak at what you've written. Your "List the rewards" of not arguing reads: "Become a bigger person. Become more compassionate to other people's feelings." You get nervous. Such lofty thoughts . . .

You need to make a few changes, and quickly, but it's not easy. Your voice raises an octave and you are just about to say something nasty and then you don't. It's not easy, but you listen instead. Her voice softens. Hey, this is getting exciting. You both exchange a few kind words. You are stunned. What's going on? You are uncomfortable. That's what risking does.

Taking risks reverses the familiar. It brings you to the edge of yourself. When you let go of your old behaviors you encounter an unknown zone. You suddenly have more options, and perhaps you don't recognize yourself for a few minutes. Take a chance! Toss away those disguises! Get real!

Risks are physical and psychological challenges. They push us to our limits in just about every way possible. Adrenaline rushes through our body when we jump off a cliff. Our hearts pound loudly when we tell someone the truth. No matter the risk, we usually feel it, and the feeling is strong. It fills our bodies with an obvious set of clues. We hear and sense, "Oh . . . yes . . . this is a risk." Sometimes it signals, "Warning . . . " Risks vibrate through our bodies and souls, giving us important information.

Often these are true signs of danger. Sometimes they are so exhilarating that we pay no attention and risk anyway. Some people avoid risks just to avoid the fear and feelings that seemingly spin out of control once they take that first step. Remember, fear is only useful sometimes. When threatened by a huge dinosaur it may be a good idea to stop dead in your tracks and pretend you are a rock. Fear informs your decision, and as a result you aren't eaten. But much of the time you will find yourself threatened by your own possibilities. Self-authored fear programs keep you tied and bound. Risk taking will help you break out of your prison of worn-out behavior. The more you risk the more you'll see what's really going on around you. Risk seeing more clearly. Risk actually listening, to your mate, your mother, your best friend. What have you got to lose? Too risky? You won't get lost; you'll be found.

Shake It Up

To grow and evolve requires shaking up the status quo. It implies a willingness to propel yourself (sometimes knowingly, sometimes blindly) toward a different and often better outcome. It requires the courage to say, "I need to take more risks." Lately, mouthing the one syllable word "risk" is risky. Taking risks has been getting a bad rap. It's automatically linked up with White House scandals, Wall Street mania, and unprotected sex.

The slogan "Just Say No!" has infested our personal decision making so completely that saying "Yes" feels almost illegal. We generalize. "Why not say 'No' to everything . . . just in case." So we say No, to our dreams, No to our inner yearnings. And No it is.

Risk turning the tables! Befriend risk! All risk isn't bad, dirty, or dangerous. Reclaim its power and value! Risk doing what you've been putting off all these years. Say "Yes" to those passions and inklings simmering on the back burner. Think about it. When you realize you won't live forever, what pops to mind that needs to get done? Have to travel? Risk going to Tibet. Learn a musical instrument? Risk playing the piano. Stop balking and start risking. If not now, when? Sometimes not risking is a bigger risk than actually making that big move.

Joe gave up a ranch he had fixed up and put all his savings into because he was determined to pursue his "mission." He wanted to become a photojournalist. "It was a calling that was bigger than me. It ignited a passion I hadn't felt since I was a kid. I threw all caution to the wind and really just risked big. Everyone told me I was a lunatic. They couldn't believe I was leaving my land and my quiet, "perfect" life. It was scary to let go of what I had known for so many years. It was a huge sense of loss, but I had to do it. I traveled the world with almost no money, collecting images and just had no idea if it would turn into anything. Was it a reckless or dangerous risk? I don't think so. I would have sat on my porch and gone silently crazy if I didn't take off."

Personal Risks

When you were a kid you probably had a few wide-eyed dreams about your future. Flying a small airplane over tropical islands? Diving for exotic creatures in the Great Barrier Reef? Exploring the stars and maybe even living on one? So much of that colorful stuff gets left behind as we grow up, filed under "Impossible." But every now and then, those yearnings pop up in the form of an urge to "do something" we often label " crazy." How do you jump out of an airplane when you have to get to the office? How do you reconcile being a successful caterer with deep-seated desires to go back to school to become a vet?

This is great material for the final chapter in *Risk Your Self,* called Personal Risks. Although it may seem a bit of a stretch to align your ordinary life with the urge to become an artist painting landscapes from a château in the Alps, *Risk Your Self* gives you full permission to at least risk taking it to heart. You deserve it. Personal Risks is the place to enter and list all of those forgotten dreams. You may find they aren't so crazy after all.

List all the risks you wish you'd have taken.
- Going to live on a kibbutz when I was nineteen
- Moving to Hawaii and living on the beach
- Teaching art in south Australia
- Becoming a ballerina
- Going to Europe with my friend Yasmin and her mother, Rita Hayward

- Going to Harvard for college
- Demanding a horse when I was young
- Learning to play the timpani drums and joining the orchestra
- Never cutting my hair so it would be long
- Becoming a photojournalist and traveling the world
- Going to guerrilla warfare school during the Vietnam era so I could "fight the revolution" at home
- Working with Gloria Steinem at *Ms.* magazine
- Moving in with a man I loved

Risk Showing Up

Taking risks is really about showing up, for yourself, for other people, or for the world. It's about being your most creative, your bravest, and your best. Fill in the blanks in *Risk Your Self* and launch yourself on a passionate journey. And don't worry, you won't lose the zest or thrill that comes with taking those first conscious risks. One risk leads to another, and multiple risks will never dampen the exhilaration of the experience.

Risk taking is a reflection of being yourself. Responding deeply and honestly to your own needs, hopes, and dreams always feels exciting. Because being fully alive is exciting, risk, and risk often. You'll fuel your imagination and inject your life decisions with more confidence, enthusiasm, and vitality.

When asked their biggest regrets at the end of their lives, many people answer, "I wish I had taken more risks." If you are looking for perfect safety, you may as well sit on a fence and watch life go by. But if you wish to live life with fewer regrets and more self-knowledge, embrace *Risk Your Self* and get your feet wet. How you show up in this book is how you show up in your life. With a little practice, you'll discover what is possible for you is way beyond your wildest imagination.

So step outside of your familiar neighborhood of limitations and habitual do's and don'ts. Risk leaving the humdrum of everyday to enter a richer realm of living life to the fullest. Remember, these are risky times and you will never know what fortunes the oceans may bring if you don't risk losing sight of the shore. *Risk Your Self* will challenge your limits but will keep you safe as you explore the waters.

Risk doing it now. If you are willing to run the risk, you will have great adventures in your life. It's worth it. Come alive and stay alive. No need to make any excuses. Yesterday was not a better time. Neither is tomorrow. *Risk Your Self*, today.

How to Use This Book

There are a number of easy and effective ways to get the most out of *Risk Your Self*. Feel free to change your approach from day to day.

• Random (drop in . . .)

Just open the book anywhere and choose a risk challenge that speaks to you.

• Special Interest (find your calling . . .)

If you have a special area of interest, you'll find many risk taking scenarios in Real Risks that titillate, elicit, conjure, or inspire you. There are eight big topics: Personal, Deep Self, Family, Change, Money, Mind-set, Adventure, and the World. Choose the topic that reflects today's passion and find a scenario that fits your needs.

• Step by Step (moving through . . .)

Take these six easy steps and move from one level of risk taking to the next:

1. Get your feet wet by filling in the risk lists in the Everyday Risks section. You'll discover your current risk taking aptitude and your risk taking history.

2. Dive into Real Risks if you want to work more complex risk challenges. You'll really get to know the pros and cons of personal change. Choose a topic that appeals to you, and start writing. Your areas of interest will change daily, so be flexible and try them all.

3. Take a chance and try Risking the Truth. This is the ultimate risk.

4. Have fun with Fantasy Risks and stretch your imagination.

5. Explore Personal Risks if you need help focusing on today's important life decision. Just fill in your challenge in the blank space provided and "work it." Think of this section as a shortcut to keeping a journal, a place to process some of what you are going through that needs clarification and movement.

Five Levels of Risk Taking

All of the risk challenges in *Risk Your Self* give you the opportunity to list the answers to a set of simple questions. Remember, risk taking challenges are designed with the belief that you can actually "do" the risks on paper first and in real life later. Whether you actually risk risking, the process will inspire you to open up your mind and clarify your decision making ability.

Chapter One: Everyday Risks are easy risks, risks you can take in a day. You simply list the risks in the left column, your thoughts, fears, and excuses that might stand in the way of movement, and list the rewards in the right column, what might happen, what you might discover, the payoff.

Chapter Two: Real Risks take a little more thought and a little more listing. Each real risk includes blank lines for a thorough process of listing: list the risks, list the worst scenario, list the rewards, list what you are willing to do. It gives you a chance not only to consider a risk in depth, but also really detail your action steps— a tangible map, a game plan . . . if you dare!

Chapter Three: Fantasy Risks are full of provocative, fun, risk taking scenarios to propel you into your imagination and escapist fantasies.

Chapter Four: Risking the Truth gives you the chance to speak your mind. You can get it off your chest and then evaluate the results.

Chapter Five: Personal Risks follows the same format as Real Risks, but offers a place to customize your own unique risk challenges.

Risk Warm-ups

Now if you want to just get started, here's a place to practice risk listing. Fill in the following Risk Lists and start building that risk taking muscle. Here's one of ours:

List some of the risks you took growing up.

- I risked burying my fifth-grade workbook in the dirt and simply didn't do the work.
- I risked asking another guy's girlfriend to go steady and she did.
- I risked not having a bar mitzvah when everyone else was.
- I risked being in a rock band that played Frank Zappa music before it was cool.
- I risked wearing painted shoes and ties and jackets to school.
- I risked going downtown on the bus to see how other people lived.
- I risked being in the "Purple Sting Ray" gang and got a bad reputation.

Now it's your turn:

- List some of the risks you took growing up.
- List the ways risk taking makes you feel.
- List what you risked today.
- List the risks you regret not having taken.
- List all the risks you have avoided taking so far.
- List all your usual reasons and excuses for not risking.

- List the risks you saw your parents take in their lives.
- List the risks you've taken in the last five years.
- List the craziest risks you have taken.
- List all the risks you'd take if you had the time, money, and courage.
- List the people you admire who've taken risks.

List the people you admire who've taken risks.

Muhammad Ali

Mother Teresa

John Cassavetes

Angela Davis

My friend Tom

Frank Zappa

The Dalai Lama

John Glenn

Walt Disney

Bob Dylan

Mikhail Gorbachev

My dad

All artists

Emergency room doctors

When to Use This Book

Use *Risk Your Self* when you are feeling out of energy, uninspired, stuck in humdrum routines, when life lacks sparkle, when you're out of sorts, bored, tired, or worn-out.

Use *Risk Your Self* when you are feeling enthusiastic, curious, wonderful, motivated, eager, wild, loose, or full of yourself.

In other words, *Risk Your Self* is a good idea all of the time. Especially . . .

- If you are in a life transition (getting married, getting divorced, graduating, moving, having a baby, and so on) it can help you sort out your options and give you clarity.

- If you are in a depression it can help you find your way out.

- If you are in limbo it can help you focus on what's truly important.

- If life throws you a curve and you suddenly need to make up your mind about something or you need to figure out what the best action is.

Risk Taking Tips

- Write fast. Do one risk in one sitting. Or . . .

- Take your time. Indulge in considering every facet of your choices.

- Write no matter what your mood. If you are frustrated or angry, so much the better.

- Writing it down helps clarify your thoughts and even the stuff you don't know you've been thinking or feeling. Hopes and dreams show up on paper. If you are in doubt, write it down anyway.

- There are really no rules except to explore with an open mind, tell the truth, and to fill in all the blanks you can . . . for now. You may return at a later date to fill in more. You'll get better at this as you go along.

- Commit to following your action steps. That means *actually taking* a risk at least once a month.

- One risk leads to another.

However and whenever you choose to risk, feel free to explore at your own pace and in your own way. Trusting yourself to know what to do and how to do it is a rather big risk in itself. Remember, writing it down always clarifies your thoughts and feelings. Pick up your pen and risk finding out what is truly important to you, today.

CHAPTER ONE
Everyday Risks

Risk not wearing a watch.

List the Risks	List the Rewards
I'll be late and get in trouble.	I may feel somewhat freer.
I'll have to actually talk to someone and I usually don't.	I may learn to trust myself more.
I always wear a watch. I'll feel naked.	I may discover I have a good sense of internal time.
I'll feel irresponsible.	I may take the time to stop and smell the roses.
My whole day will fall apart.	Change is good. So is a new perspective.
I won't know what time it is.	I'll stop staring at my watch all day long and feeling like I'm not doing enough.

EVERYDAY
Risks

Everyday risks are quick warm-ups designed to wake up your risk taking muscle. At first glance they may appear a little quirky, not so risky, but interesting. These are easy risks, but they have more impact than you think. Everyday risks give you a solid peek into the power and control you have over your own life.

For example, "Risk staying in bed all day on Sunday" might seem like a no-brainer. Just do it, right? Not exactly. As you list the risks you find yourself admitting you don't feel worthy, you're worried what your friends might think, and so it goes. You thought your life was your own, huh, but is it really?

Or consider "Risk taking a different route home from work" or "Risk singing out loud." Everyday risks will actually introduce you to a whole new world, without much effort. You'll be amazed at how making minor changes in your daily habits will affect how you feel about yourself and your daily grind. You may discover the comfort zone you inhabit is actually more rut than sanctuary.

And what about the potential rewards of, say, "Risk not wearing a watch for one day." Refer to the completed sample and scan the "responses." Under "List the Rewards ..." you'll notice six revelations listed that express how not wearing a watch might make a difference. They include developing a deeper sense of self-trust as well as simply feeling freer. Something as banal a putting the Timex on the dresser for twenty-four hours is really not as ho-hum as you think. Just musing about making these small changes in your life will give you permission to imagine much bigger possibilities.

Try filling in two Everyday Risk challenges each week for a month and keep track of the results. If you feel brave or just plain curious, take one of your favorite risks off the page and into your life. Why not "Risk going barefoot all day"? Just leave your shoes by the door—take a chance. Remember, these risks are doable and fun. Let Everyday Risks open your eyes and whet your whistle to the more daunting risks ahead.

Risk helping a stranger.

List the Risks   List the Rewards

_____   _____

_____   _____

_____   _____

_____   _____

_____   _____

_____   _____

_____   _____

_____   _____

Risk being an organ donor.

List the Risks   List the Rewards

_____   _____

_____   _____

_____   _____

_____   _____

_____   _____

_____   _____

_____   _____

_____   _____

Risk saying "I don't know."

List the Risks   List the Rewards

_____   _____

_____   _____

_____   _____

_____   _____

_____   _____

_____   _____

_____   _____

_____   _____

Risk looking someone in the eye.

List the Risks   List the Rewards

_____   _____

_____   _____

_____   _____

_____   _____

_____   _____

_____   _____

_____   _____

Risk building something by hand.

List the Risks   List the Rewards

Risk not biting your nails.

List the Risks   List the Rewards

Risk staying in bed all day on Sunday.

List the Risks   List the Rewards

_____   _____

_____   _____

_____   _____

_____   _____

_____   _____

_____   _____

_____   _____

Risk writing an erotic poem.

List the Risks   List the Rewards

_____   _____

_____   _____

_____   _____

_____   _____

_____   _____

_____   _____

_____   _____

Risk going barefoot all day.

List the Risks   List the Rewards

_____   _____

_____   _____

_____   _____

_____   _____

_____   _____

_____   _____

_____   _____

_____   _____

Risk taking a bubble bath
in the middle of the day.

List the Risks   List the Rewards

_____   _____

_____   _____

_____   _____

_____   _____

_____   _____

_____   _____

_____   _____

Risk standing on your head.

List the Risks   List the Rewards

_____   _____

_____   _____

_____   _____

_____   _____

_____   _____

_____   _____

_____   _____

_____   _____

Risk talking deeply with your mother or father.

List the Risks   List the Rewards

_____   _____

_____   _____

_____   _____

_____   _____

_____   _____

_____   _____

_____   _____

Risk making love outside under the stars.

List the Risks   List the Rewards

_____   _____

_____   _____

_____   _____

_____   _____

_____   _____

_____   _____

_____   _____

_____   _____

Risk rolling in mud.

List the Risks   List the Rewards

_____   _____

_____   _____

_____   _____

_____   _____

_____   _____

_____   _____

_____   _____

Risk giving up coffee.

List the Risks   List the Rewards

_____   _____

_____   _____

_____   _____

_____   _____

_____   _____

_____   _____

_____   _____

_____   _____

Risk swimming with dolphins.

List the Risks   List the Rewards

_____   _____

_____   _____

_____   _____

_____   _____

_____   _____

_____   _____

_____   _____

Risk not watching TV.

List the Risks   List the Rewards

_____   _____

_____   _____

_____   _____

_____   _____

_____   _____

_____   _____

_____   _____

_____   _____

Risk dancing all night.

List the Risks   List the Rewards

_____   _____

_____   _____

_____   _____

_____   _____

_____   _____

_____   _____

_____   _____

Risk *not* procrastinating.

List the Risks   List the Rewards

_____   _____

_____   _____

_____   _____

_____   _____

_____   _____

_____   _____

_____   _____

_____   _____

Risk not making excuses for other people.

List the Risks   List the Rewards

_____   _____

_____   _____

_____   _____

_____   _____

_____   _____

_____   _____

_____   _____

Risk living without envy.

List the Risks	List the Rewards

Risk eating anything you want for one day.

List the Risks	List the Rewards

Risk being on time.

List the Risks   List the Rewards

Risk cleaning out your attic, garage, closets, or brain.

List the Risks   List the Rewards

Risk dressing in a style you're just not used to.

List the Risks   List the Rewards

_____   _____

_____   _____

_____   _____

_____   _____

_____   _____

_____   _____

_____   _____

_____   _____

Risk not caring about money for a week.

List the Risks   List the Rewards

_____   _____

_____   _____

_____   _____

_____   _____

_____   _____

_____   _____

_____   _____

Risk making a fool out of yourself.

List the Risks   List the Rewards

_____   _____

_____   _____

_____   _____

_____   _____

_____   _____

_____   _____

_____   _____

_____   _____

Risk weeping over something small.

List the Risks   List the Rewards

_____   _____

_____   _____

_____   _____

_____   _____

_____   _____

_____   _____

_____   _____

Risk expressing your ideas before a crowd.

List the Risks   List the Rewards

_____   _____
_____   _____
_____   _____
_____   _____
_____   _____
_____   _____
_____   _____
_____   _____

Risk waking one hour early
just to spend time with yourself.

List the Risks   List the Rewards

_____   _____
_____   _____
_____   _____
_____   _____
_____   _____
_____   _____
_____   _____

Risk asking for help or advice about everything.

List the Risks   List the Rewards

_____   _____

_____   _____

_____   _____

_____   _____

_____   _____

_____   _____

_____   _____

_____   _____

Risk not checking your E-mail/ voice mail/snail mail for a day.

List the Risks   List the Rewards

_____   _____

_____   _____

_____   _____

_____   _____

_____   _____

_____   _____

_____   _____

Risk treating others like someone in your family.

List the Risks   List the Rewards

Risk going to a bookstore and spending one hour in a totally unfamiliar aisle.

List the Risks   List the Rewards

Risk taking a walk every day.

List the Risks   List the Rewards

_____   _____
_____   _____
_____   _____
_____   _____
_____   _____
_____   _____
_____   _____
_____   _____

Risk having someone else
order food for you at a restaurant.

List the Risks   List the Rewards

_____   _____
_____   _____
_____   _____
_____   _____
_____   _____
_____   _____
_____   _____

Risk painting your bedroom a wild color.

List the Risks   List the Rewards

_____   _____

_____   _____

_____   _____

_____   _____

_____   _____

_____   _____

_____   _____

Risk going out without your makeup.

List the Risks   List the Rewards

_____   _____

_____   _____

_____   _____

_____   _____

_____   _____

_____   _____

_____   _____

Risk riding a roller coaster.

List the Risks   List the Rewards

Risk eating something different for breakfast.

List the Risks   List the Rewards

Risk not driving one day a week.

List the Risks   List the Rewards

_____   _____

_____   _____

_____   _____

_____   _____

_____   _____

_____   _____

_____   _____

_____   _____

Risk finally thanking someone.

List the Risks   List the Rewards

_____   _____

_____   _____

_____   _____

_____   _____

_____   _____

_____   _____

_____   _____

Risk making a painting.

List the Risks | List the Rewards

_____ | _____
_____ | _____
_____ | _____
_____ | _____
_____ | _____
_____ | _____
_____ | _____
_____ | _____

Risk taking a different route home from work.

List the Risks | List the Rewards

_____ | _____
_____ | _____
_____ | _____
_____ | _____
_____ | _____
_____ | _____
_____ | _____

Risk learning the guitar.

List the Risks   List the Rewards

_____   _____

_____   _____

_____   _____

_____   _____

_____   _____

_____   _____

_____   _____

Risk learning to sail.

List the Risks   List the Rewards

_____   _____

_____   _____

_____   _____

_____   _____

_____   _____

_____   _____

_____   _____

Risk learning a new language.

List the Risks   List the Rewards

Risk writing your will.

List the Risks   List the Rewards

Risk balancing your checkbook.

List the Risks	List the Rewards

Risk laughing at yourself.

List the Risks	List the Rewards

Risk hugging your father.

List the Risks   List the Rewards

Risk giving away the stuff you just don't need.

List the Risks   List the Rewards

Risk showing up early.

List the Risks	List the Rewards

Risk complimenting your mother.

List the Risks	List the Rewards

Risk giving flowers to someone.

List the Risks   List the Rewards

Risk dancing in public.

List the Risks   List the Rewards

Risk talking with your neighbors.

List the Risks	List the Rewards

Risk going somewhere you've never been before.

List the Risks	List the Rewards

Risk taking a nap.

List the Risks	List the Rewards

Risk going camping.

List the Risks	List the Rewards

Risk shaving your head.

List the Risks | List the Rewards

_____ | _____

_____ | _____

_____ | _____

_____ | _____

_____ | _____

_____ | _____

_____ | _____

Risk staying up past your bedtime.

List the Risks | List the Rewards

_____ | _____

_____ | _____

_____ | _____

_____ | _____

_____ | _____

_____ | _____

_____ | _____

Risk riding a motorcycle cross-country.

List the Risks   List the Rewards

Risk changing your name.

List the Risks   List the Rewards

Risk camping alone under the full moon.

List the Risks   List the Rewards

_____   _____

_____   _____

_____   _____

_____   _____

_____   _____

_____   _____

_____   _____

_____   _____

Risk visiting that one place
you've always longed to see.

List the Risks   List the Rewards

_____   _____

_____   _____

_____   _____

_____   _____

_____   _____

_____   _____

_____   _____

_____   _____

Risk telling that one person off for good.

List the Risks

List the Rewards

Risk buying something on impulse.

List the Risks

List the Rewards

Risk giving someone another chance.

List the Risks   List the Rewards

_____   _____

_____   _____

_____   _____

_____   _____

_____   _____

_____   _____

_____   _____

_____   _____

Risk flying a kite.

List the Risks   List the Rewards

_____   _____

_____   _____

_____   _____

_____   _____

_____   _____

_____   _____

_____   _____

Risk renewing your wedding vows.

List the Risks   List the Rewards

Risk owning less.

List the Risks   List the Rewards

Risk playing hooky from work.

List the Risks | List the Rewards

Risk dining by candlelight, alone.

List the Risks | List the Rewards

EVERYDAY RISKS

Risk wearing bright red lipstick.

List the Risks   List the Rewards

Risk not doing anything
on your to-do list for a day.

List the Risks   List the Rewards

Risk not reading the newspaper for a week.

List the Risks   List the Rewards

_____   _____

_____   _____

_____   _____

_____   _____

_____   _____

_____   _____

_____   _____

Risk asking for a big favor.

List the Risks   List the Rewards

_____   _____

_____   _____

_____   _____

_____   _____

_____   _____

_____   _____

_____   _____

Risk not arguing for a day.

List the Risks   List the Rewards

_____   _____
_____   _____
_____   _____
_____   _____
_____   _____
_____   _____
_____   _____
_____   _____

Risk planting a garden.

List the Risks   List the Rewards

_____   _____
_____   _____
_____   _____
_____   _____
_____   _____
_____   _____
_____   _____

Risk watching the sunrise.

List the Risks	List the Rewards

Risk smiling at strangers.

List the Risks	List the Rewards

Risk learning to play the piano.

List the Risks   List the Rewards

_____ _____

_____ _____

_____ _____

_____ _____

_____ _____

_____ _____

_____ _____

_____ _____

Risk tasting something really new.

List the Risks   List the Rewards

_____ _____

_____ _____

_____ _____

_____ _____

_____ _____

_____ _____

_____ _____

_____ _____

Risk writing down your dreams.

List the Risks   List the Rewards

_____   _____

_____   _____

_____   _____

_____   _____

_____   _____

_____   _____

_____   _____

_____   _____

Risk swimming in the ocean.

List the Risks   List the Rewards

_____   _____

_____   _____

_____   _____

_____   _____

_____   _____

_____   _____

_____   _____

_____   _____

Risk growing your own food.

List the Risks   List the Rewards

Risk walking in the rain.

List the Risks   List the Rewards

Risk singing out loud.

List the Risks   List the Rewards

_____   _____

_____   _____

_____   _____

_____   _____

_____   _____

_____   _____

_____   _____

Risk making a budget and sticking to it.

List the Risks   List the Rewards

_____   _____

_____   _____

_____   _____

_____   _____

_____   _____

_____   _____

_____   _____

Risk having your parents over for dinner.

List the Risks

List the Rewards

_____   _____

_____   _____

_____   _____

_____   _____

_____   _____

_____   _____

_____   _____

_____   _____

Risk giving an anonymous gift.

List the Risks

List the Rewards

_____   _____

_____   _____

_____   _____

_____   _____

_____   _____

_____   _____

_____   _____

_____   _____

Risk seeing a psychic.

List the Risks   List the Rewards

_____   _____

_____   _____

_____   _____

_____   _____

_____   _____

_____   _____

_____   _____

Risk spending two hours alone in an art museum.

List the Risks   List the Rewards

_____   _____

_____   _____

_____   _____

_____   _____

_____   _____

_____   _____

_____   _____

Risk redecorating your home.

List the Risks   List the Rewards

Risk calling the person you've been avoiding.

List the Risks   List the Rewards

CHAPTER TWO
Real Risks

Risk Buying a Home

List the Risks

I'm afraid of the new neighborhood.

The value of the house might drop.

The house will be a ton of work forever.

I'll have to work more to pay the bills.

I'm afraid of taking out a loan

The house might be haunted.

I'm afraid to take on the responsibility.

List the Worst Scenario

The neighbors are insane and noisy maniacs.

I lose my job and won't be able to handle the mortgage.

I spend all my time working on the house and I have no life, no friends.

All I do is fix the house.

The market takes a dive and I can't ever get rid of it.

List the Rewards

I can do whatever I want to it.

I have equity ... maybe.

The value could double.

I have my own parking place.

I can create my own sanctuary or psychedelic retreat.

This represents growth and moving forward.

List What You Are Willing to Do

I'll call a loan broker and see.

I'll read the paper and spend a weekend looking.

I'll consider talking to my boss about job security.

I'll talk to my friends who own homes and get a taste.

I'll see who might help me with finances and advice.

REAL *Risks*

Real risks are easy to identify. They are big risks that usually involve big life transitions, like "Risk getting married," "Risk having children," "Risk changing jobs," "Risk moving out of town." They are often things you've thought about doing for years, and have put off because of a mixture of fear, apprehension, and the overwhelming impact of possible success.

For example, "Risk buying a home" means taking on a huge responsibility along with all of the wonderful benefits that go along with being a homeowner. Naturally, dread lurks in the corners of your heart and mind and you'll find that your "List the risks" will overflow with legitimate excuses and real, solid reasons not to . . . yet.

The Real Risk sample illuminates a whole batch of fears at the prospect of taking the plunge. Under "List the Worst Scenario" you are invited to expand the nightmare, fill in the blanks, and go for it. Here you see some real dread expressed, from crazy neighbors to financial demise. Of course when you look at "List the Rewards" you'll notice a solid set of payoffs, from tangible equity to the more abstract but no less viable pride of living in your own home at last.

Remember, you are taking these risks on paper, first. Under the "List What Are You Willing to Do" section you may discover an action step that pulls you off the paper and into the real world. If you feel you've processed the risk sufficiently and honestly, you may feel your risk taking muscle getting strong enough to actually take this risk out into the world.

Real Risks is divided into eight topics: Personal, Deep Self, Family, Change, Money, Mind-set, Adventure, and the World. Choose the topic that appeals to you, or do them all. You'll find out more about what makes you tick, and you'll be ready to handle the real risks that truly reflect your particular needs.

Remember, real risks can and will change your life. They allow you to finally face yourself. All the things you've dreamed of doing but have been putting off for whatever reason can be confronted, at least on paper, and dealt with. It's time to take yourself and your goals more seriously. So roll up your sleeves, take a deep breath, and risk away!

Risk falling in love.

List the Risks

List the Worst Scenario

List the Rewards

List What You Are Willing to Do

Risk being celibate for a year.

List the Risks

List the Worst Scenario

List the Rewards

List What You Are Willing to Do

Risk having the kind of sex you dream of.

List the Risks

List the Worst Scenario

List the Rewards

List What You Are Willing to Do

Risk loving who you see in the mirror.

List the Risks

List the Worst Scenario

_____

_____

_____

_____

_____

_____

_____

_____

List the Rewards

List What You Are Willing to Do

_____

_____

_____

_____

_____

_____

_____

_____

Risk taking care of your own needs first.

List the Risks

_____

_____

_____

_____

_____

_____

_____

List the Worst Scenario

_____

_____

_____

_____

_____

_____

List the Rewards

_____

_____

_____

_____

_____

_____

List What You Are Willing to Do

_____

_____

_____

_____

_____

_____

Risk not feeling sorry for yourself.

List the Risks

_____

_____

_____

_____

_____

_____

_____

List the Worst Scenario

_____

_____

_____

_____

_____

_____

_____

List the Rewards

_____

_____

_____

_____

_____

_____

_____

List What You Are Willing to Do

_____

_____

_____

_____

_____

_____

_____

Risk keeping your mouth shut.

List the Risks

List the Worst Scenario

List the Rewards

List What You Are Willing to Do

Risk saying "I'm sorry."

List the Risks

List the Worst Scenario

_____

_____

_____

_____

_____

_____

_____

_____

_____

List the Rewards

List What You Are Willing to Do

_____

_____

_____

_____

_____

_____

_____

_____

Risk not worrying.

List the Risks

List the Worst Scenario

List the Rewards

List What You Are Willing to Do

Risk living without regrets.

List the Risks

List the Worst Scenario

List the Rewards

List What You Are Willing to Do

Risk cleaning up your act.

List the Risks

List the Worst Scenario

List the Rewards

List What You Are Willing to Do

Risk breaking the rules.

List the Risks   List the Worst Scenario

_____   _____

_____   _____

_____   _____

_____   _____

_____   _____

_____   _____

_____   _____

List the Rewards   List What You Are Willing to Do

_____   _____

_____   _____

_____   _____

_____   _____

_____   _____

_____   _____

Risk patting yourself on the back.

List the Risks

List the Worst Scenario

List the Rewards

List What You Are Willing to Do

Risk not pleasing everyone all the time.

List the Risks

List the Worst Scenario

List the Rewards

List What You Are Willing to Do

Risk being different.

List the Risks

List the Worst Scenario

List the Rewards

List What You Are Willing to Do

Risk setting and keeping boundaries.

List the Risks

List the Worst Scenario

List the Rewards

List What You Are Willing to Do

Risk crying in public.

List the Risks

List the Worst Scenario

List the Rewards

List What You Are Willing to Do

Risk revealing a deep secret.

List the Risks

List the Worst Scenario

List the Rewards

List What You Are Willing to Do

Risk trusting someone completely.

List the Risks

List the Worst Scenario

List the Rewards

List What You Are Willing to Do

Risk telling the people you know how you really feel.

List the Risks

List the Worst Scenario

List the Rewards

List What You Are Willing to Do

Risk excelling despite your handicaps.

List the Risks

List the Worst Scenario

List the Rewards

List What You Are Willing to Do

Risk believing you are loved.

List the Risks

List the Worst Scenario

List the Rewards

List What You Are Willing to Do

Risk being depressed and not running from it.

List the Risks

_____

_____

_____

_____

_____

_____

_____

List the Worst Scenario

_____

_____

_____

_____

_____

_____

_____

List the Rewards

_____

_____

_____

_____

_____

_____

_____

List What You Are Willing to Do

_____

_____

_____

_____

_____

_____

_____

Risk expressing your rage.

List the Risks   List the Worst Scenario

_____   _____
_____   _____
_____   _____
_____   _____
_____   _____
_____   _____
_____   _____
_____   _____

List the Rewards   List What You Are Willing to Do

_____   _____
_____   _____
_____   _____
_____   _____
_____   _____
_____   _____
_____   _____

Risk putting the past behind you.

List the Risks

List the Worst Scenario

List the Rewards

List What You Are Willing to Do

Risk talking to God.

List the Risks   List the Worst Scenario

_____   _____

_____   _____

_____   _____

_____   _____

_____   _____

_____   _____

_____   _____

_____   _____

List the Rewards   List What You Are Willing to Do

_____   _____

_____   _____

_____   _____

_____   _____

_____   _____

_____   _____

_____   _____

Risk being happy.

List the Risks

List the Worst Scenario

List the Rewards

List What You Are Willing to Do

Risk finding your inner peace.

List the Risks   List the Worst Scenario

_____   _____

_____   _____

_____   _____

_____   _____

_____   _____

_____   _____

_____   _____

_____   _____

List the Rewards   List What You Are Willing to Do

_____   _____

_____   _____

_____   _____

_____   _____

_____   _____

_____   _____

_____   _____

Risk believing you are not alone.

List the Risks

List the Worst Scenario

List the Rewards

List What You Are Willing to Do

Risk discovering your higher purpose.

List the Risks

List the Worst Scenario

List the Rewards

List What You Are Willing to Do

Risk saying "I love you" to your mother or father.

List the Risks

List the Worst Scenario

List the Rewards

List What You Are Willing to Do

Risk taking time off from your career to be with your kids.

List the Risks

List the Worst Scenario

List the Rewards

List What You Are Willing to Do

Risk celebrating a holiday without feeling obligated to spend it with your family.

List the Risks

List the Worst Scenario

List the Rewards

List What You Are Willing to Do

Risk having children.

List the Risks

List the Worst Scenario

List the Rewards

List What You Are Willing to Do

Risk not having children.

List the Risks

List the Worst Scenario

List the Rewards

List What You Are Willing to Do

Risk disagreeing with your spouse.

List the Risks

List the Worst Scenario

List the Rewards

List What You Are Willing to Do

Risk taking care of your aging parents.

List the Risks

List the Worst Scenario

List the Rewards

List What You Are Willing to Do

Risk having a really honest conversation with your parents.

List the Risks

List the Worst Scenario

List the Rewards

List What You Are Willing to Do

Risk reconnecting with your estranged parent/husband/wife/other.

List the Risks

List the Worst Scenario

List the Rewards

List What You Are Willing to Do

Risk moving to the country to raise your kids.

List the Risks

List the Worst Scenario

List the Rewards

List What You Are Willing to Do

Risk saying *no* to your husband, boss, or mother.

List the Risks

List the Worst Scenario

List the Rewards

List What You Are Willing to Do

Risk putting your marriage first.

List the Risks   List the Worst Scenario

_____   _____
_____   _____
_____   _____
_____   _____
_____   _____
_____   _____
_____   _____
_____   _____

List the Rewards   List What You Are Willing to Do

_____   _____
_____   _____
_____   _____
_____   _____
_____   _____
_____   _____
_____   _____

Risk losing weight.

List the Risks

List the Worst Scenario

List the Rewards

List What You Are Willing to Do

Risk being openly gay.

List the Risks

List the Worst Scenario

List the Rewards

List What You Are Willing to Do

Risk leaving a relationship that isn't nurturing.

List the Risks

_____

_____

_____

_____

_____

_____

_____

_____

List the Worst Scenario

_____

_____

_____

_____

_____

_____

_____

List the Rewards

_____

_____

_____

_____

_____

_____

_____

_____

List What You Are Willing to Do

_____

_____

_____

_____

_____

_____

_____

_____

Risk letting your hair go gray.

List the Risks

List the Worst Scenario

List the Rewards

List What You Are Willing to Do

Risk going to your high school reunion.

List the Risks   List the Worst Scenario

_____   _____

_____   _____

_____   _____

_____   _____

_____   _____

_____   _____

_____   _____

_____   _____

List the Rewards   List What You Are Willing to Do

_____   _____

_____   _____

_____   _____

_____   _____

_____   _____

_____   _____

_____   _____

Risk weeding out your friends.

List the Risks

List the Worst Scenario

List the Rewards

List What You Are Willing to Do

Risk quitting your job, today.

List the Risks

List the Worst Scenario

List the Rewards

List What You Are Willing to Do

Risk converting to a more meaningful religion.

List the Risks

List the Worst Scenario

List the Rewards

List What You Are Willing to Do

Risk getting married.

List the Risks

List the Worst Scenario

List the Rewards

List What You Are Willing to Do

Risk changing careers.

List the Risks

List the Worst Scenario

List the Rewards

List What You Are Willing to Do

Risk moving to a new city.

List the Risks

List the Worst Scenario

List the Rewards

List What You Are Willing to Do

Risk getting a face-lift.

List the Risks

List the Worst Scenario

_____

_____

_____

_____

_____

_____

_____

List the Rewards

List What You Are Willing to Do

_____

_____

_____

_____

_____

_____

_____

Risk getting divorced.

List the Risks

_____

_____

_____

_____

_____

_____

_____

List the Worst Scenario

_____

_____

_____

_____

_____

_____

_____

List the Rewards

_____

_____

_____

_____

_____

_____

_____

List What You Are Willing to Do

_____

_____

_____

_____

_____

_____

_____

Risk going back to school and beginning again.

List the Risks

List the Worst Scenario

List the Rewards

List What You Are Willing to Do

Risk writing and mailing that important letter.

List the Risks

List the Worst Scenario

List the Rewards

List What You Are Willing to Do

Risk embracing a regular health regime.

List the Risks

List the Worst Scenario

List the Rewards

List What You Are Willing to Do

Risk saying good-bye for good.

List the Risks   List the Worst Scenario

List the Rewards   List What You Are Willing to Do

Risk bringing a new pet into your home.

List the Risks

List the Worst Scenario

List the Rewards

List What You Are Willing to Do

Risk getting involved with some unfamiliar project to enrich your life.

List the Risks

List the Worst Scenario

List the Rewards

List What You Are Willing to Do

Risk borrowing money from a loved one.

List the Risks

List the Worst Scenario

List the Rewards

List What You Are Willing to Do

Risk starting your own business.

List the Risks

_____

_____

_____

_____

_____

_____

_____

List the Worst Scenario

_____

_____

_____

_____

_____

_____

_____

List the Rewards

_____

_____

_____

_____

_____

_____

_____

List What You Are Willing to Do

_____

_____

_____

_____

_____

_____

_____

Risk buying a home.

List the Risks

List the Worst Scenario

List the Rewards

List What You Are Willing to Do

Risk writing that check.

List the Risks

List the Worst Scenario

_____

_____

_____

_____

_____

_____

_____

List the Rewards

List What You Are Willing to Do

_____

_____

_____

_____

_____

_____

_____

Risk being really generous.

List the Risks

List the Worst Scenario

List the Rewards

List What You Are Willing to Do

Risk asking for money you've been owed.

List the Risks

List the Worst Scenario

List the Rewards

List What You Are Willing to Do

Risk asking for that raise.

List the Risks   List the Worst Scenario

_____   _____
_____   _____
_____   _____
_____   _____
_____   _____
_____   _____
_____   _____
_____   _____

List the Rewards   List What You Are Willing to Do

_____   _____
_____   _____
_____   _____
_____   _____
_____   _____
_____   _____
_____   _____

Risk being extravagant.

List the Risks   List the Worst Scenario

List the Rewards   List What You Are Willing to Do

Risk working with your mate.

List the Risks

List the Worst Scenario

_____

_____

_____

_____

_____

_____

_____

List the Rewards

List What You Are Willing to Do

_____

_____

_____

_____

_____

_____

_____

Risk playing the stock market.

List the Risks

List the Worst Scenario

_____

_____

_____

_____

_____

_____

_____

List the Rewards

List What You Are Willing to Do

_____

_____

_____

_____

_____

_____

_____

Risk going bankrupt.

List the Risks

List the Worst Scenario

_____

_____

_____

_____

_____

_____

_____

_____

List the Rewards

List What You Are Willing to Do

_____

_____

_____

_____

_____

_____

_____

_____

Risk taking out a loan.

List the Risks

List the Worst Scenario

List the Rewards

List What You Are Willing to Do

Risk paying off your debts.

List the Risks

List the Worst Scenario

List the Rewards

List What You Are Willing to Do

Risk being self-sufficient.

List the Risks

List the Worst Scenario

List the Rewards

List What You Are Willing to Do

Risk carrying out just one
of your million-dollar ideas.

List the Risks   List the Worst Scenario

_____   _____

_____   _____

_____   _____

_____   _____

_____   _____

_____   _____

_____   _____

List the Rewards   List What You Are Willing to Do

_____   _____

_____   _____

_____   _____

_____   _____

_____   _____

_____   _____

_____   _____

Risk sinking all your savings into a friend's new business.

List the Risks

List the Worst Scenario

_____

_____

_____

_____

_____

_____

_____

List the Rewards

List What You Are Willing to Do

_____

_____

_____

_____

_____

_____

_____

Risk gambling with your recent earnings.

List the Risks

List the Worst Scenario

List the Rewards

List What You Are Willing to Do

Risk mastering one thing completely.

List the Risks

List the Worst Scenario

_____

_____

_____

_____

_____

_____

_____

List the Rewards

List What You Are Willing to Do

_____

_____

_____

_____

_____

_____

_____

Risk living your life like this year is your last.

List the Risks

List the Worst Scenario

_____

_____

_____

_____

_____

_____

_____

_____

List the Rewards

List What You Are Willing to Do

_____

_____

_____

_____

_____

_____

_____

Risk doing what you love every day.

List the Risks

_____

_____

_____

_____

_____

_____

_____

List the Worst Scenario

_____

_____

_____

_____

_____

_____

_____

List the Rewards

_____

_____

_____

_____

_____

_____

_____

List What You Are Willing to Do

_____

_____

_____

_____

_____

_____

_____

Risk listening to and acting on your instincts.

List the Risks   List the Worst Scenario

_____   _____

_____   _____

_____   _____

_____   _____

_____   _____

_____   _____

_____   _____

List the Rewards   List What You Are Willing to Do

_____   _____

_____   _____

_____   _____

_____   _____

_____   _____

_____   _____

_____   _____

Risk not gossiping.

List the Risks

List the Worst Scenario

_____

_____

_____

_____

_____

_____

_____

List the Rewards

List What You Are Willing to Do

_____

_____

_____

_____

_____

_____

_____

Risk sleeping alone and liking it.

List the Risks

List the Worst Scenario

List the Rewards

List What You Are Willing to Do

Risk meditating daily.

List the Risks

List the Worst Scenario

List the Rewards

List What You Are Willing to Do

Risk breaking one truly bad habit.

List the Risks

List the Worst Scenario

List the Rewards

List What You Are Willing to Do

Risk getting organized.

List the Risks

List the Worst Scenario

List the Rewards

List What You Are Willing to Do

Risk asking more stupid questions.

List the Risks

List the Worst Scenario

List the Rewards

List What You Are Willing to Do

Risk not lying.

List the Risks

List the Worst Scenario

List the Rewards

List What You Are Willing to Do

Risk adopting a new good habit, one that you've always wanted.

List the Risks

_____

_____

_____

_____

_____

_____

_____

List the Worst Scenario

_____

_____

_____

_____

_____

_____

List the Rewards

_____

_____

_____

_____

_____

_____

_____

List What You Are Willing to Do

_____

_____

_____

_____

_____

_____

_____

Risk living without electricity
or a telephone in your home.

List the Risks

List the Worst Scenario

List the Rewards

List What You Are Willing to Do

Risk being an artist.

List the Risks

List the Worst Scenario

List the Rewards

List What You Are Willing to Do

Risk doing what you fear the most.

List the Risks

List the Worst Scenario

List the Rewards

List What You Are Willing to Do

Risk getting a pilot's license.

List the Risks

List the Worst Scenario

List the Rewards

List What You Are Willing to Do

Risk dropping out and traveling for a year.

List the Risks

List the Worst Scenario

List the Rewards

List What You Are Willing to Do

Risk trying an extremely challenging sport.

List the Risks   List the Worst Scenario

_____   _____
_____   _____
_____   _____
_____   _____
_____   _____
_____   _____
_____   _____

List the Rewards   List What You Are Willing to Do

_____   _____
_____   _____
_____   _____
_____   _____
_____   _____
_____   _____
_____   _____

Risk running a marathon.

List the Risks

List the Worst Scenario

List the Rewards

List What You Are Willing to Do

Risk camping alone in a remote spot.

List the Risks

List the Worst Scenario

List the Rewards

List What You Are Willing to Do

Risk white-water rafting or scaling a mountain.

List the Risks

List the Worst Scenario

List the Rewards

List What You Are Willing to Do

Risk taking that dream trip, at last.

List the Risks   List the Worst Scenario

_____   _____
_____   _____
_____   _____
_____   _____
_____   _____
_____   _____
_____   _____
_____   _____

List the Rewards   List What You Are Willing to Do

_____   _____
_____   _____
_____   _____
_____   _____
_____   _____
_____   _____
_____   _____

Risk visiting the town where you grew up.

List the Risks

List the Worst Scenario

List the Rewards

List What You Are Willing to Do

Risk going somewhere, anywhere, all by yourself.

List the Risks	List the Worst Scenario

List the Rewards	List What You Are Willing to Do

Risk retreating from the world for a while.

List the Risks

_____

_____

_____

_____

_____

_____

_____

List the Worst Scenario

_____

_____

_____

_____

_____

_____

_____

List the Rewards

_____

_____

_____

_____

_____

_____

_____

List What You Are Willing to Do

_____

_____

_____

_____

_____

_____

_____

Risk being silent for an entire week.

List the Risks

List the Worst Scenario

List the Rewards

List What You Are Willing to Do

Risk living abroad.

List the Risks

List the Worst Scenario

List the Rewards

List What You Are Willing to Do

Risk leaving home.

List the Risks

List the Worst Scenario

List the Rewards

List What You Are Willing to Do

Risk closing your eyes, pointing to a spot on the map, and going there.

List the Risks

List the Worst Scenario

List the Rewards

List What You Are Willing to Do

Risk running for public office.

List the Risks

List the Worst Scenario

List the Rewards

List What You Are Willing to Do

Risk learning CPR.

List the Risks

List the Worst Scenario

_____

_____

_____

_____

_____

_____

_____

_____

List the Rewards

List What You Are Willing to Do

_____

_____

_____

_____

_____

_____

_____

_____

Risk adopting a child.

List the Risks

List the Worst Scenario

List the Rewards

List What You Are Willing to Do

Risk donating your time.

List the Risks

List the Worst Scenario

List the Rewards

List What You Are Willing to Do

Risk forgiving your enemies.

List the Risks

List the Worst Scenario

List the Rewards

List What You Are Willing to Do

Risk not hating.

List the Risks

List the Worst Scenario

_____

_____

_____

_____

_____

_____

_____

List the Rewards

List What You Are Willing to Do

_____

_____

_____

_____

_____

_____

_____

Risk being a hero.

List the Risks

List the Worst Scenario

List the Rewards

List What You Are Willing to Do

Risk asking forgiveness of everyone you have hurt.

List the Risks

_____

_____

_____

_____

_____

_____

_____

List the Worst Scenario

_____

_____

_____

_____

_____

_____

_____

List the Rewards

_____

_____

_____

_____

_____

_____

_____

List What You Are Willing to Do

_____

_____

_____

_____

_____

_____

_____

Risk living without envy.

List the Risks

List the Worst Scenario

List the Rewards

List What You Are Willing to Do

Risk taking a stand on political issues.

List the Risks

List the Worst Scenario

List the Rewards

List What You Are Willing to Do

Risk getting involved in a charity or social cause.

List the Risks

_____

_____

_____

_____

_____

_____

_____

_____

List the Worst Scenario

_____

_____

_____

_____

_____

_____

_____

_____

List the Rewards

_____

_____

_____

_____

_____

_____

_____

List What You Are Willing to Do

_____

_____

_____

_____

_____

_____

_____

Risk giving away everything
that you don't use or need.

List the Risks

List the Worst Scenario

List the Rewards

List What You Are Willing to Do

CHAPTER THREE
Fantasy Risks

*Y*ou have just won $3 million from the lottery. This lottery, however, is different. You cannot use the money unless you spend all of your winnings to improve the environment (plants, animals, trees, habitats) or to help other people or less fortunate nations. You have two months to do this or you lose the opportunity.

List What You Would Do

I'd spend a good two weeks researching the most legitimate causes and organizations and compile a list. I'd immediately send $1,000,000 to Save Tibet for the children in the orphanages. I'd take $1,000,000 and invest it in solid, earth-loving stocks. I'd divide up the rest of the money for refuge funds, wildlife preservation, and serious environmental foundations.

List Any Secret Fears

I'd realize this money will hardly touch the problems and I'll become saddened. I'll realize some charities might not do what they claim, and I'd have to face corruption in the places I'd like to think everything was dandy. I might make some mistakes and that will hurt. People that I know might be angry with me because I don't support their cause and that might alienate us.

List How This Event Might Help or Affect Your Life Now

I'd be launched immediately into a bigger vision of myself and my place in the world. I'd see how hard it is to do the right thing. I would get a feeling of personal satisfaction that I made a difference. I'd take on a responsibility beyond my daily concerns that would enlarge me as a human and hopefully make me more loving and compassionate.

FANTASY
Risks

Fantasy risks are fun, a chance to kick back and play a little. Suspend the "How could I?" and "That's impossible" responses. This is time to stretch a little. You may wonder how a fantasy could be risky. The truth is, most of us edit our daydreams, limit our visions, squelch our creativity. Why? Because our imaginations threaten to get us in trouble. They can easily upset our busy lives by turning the status quo upside down! And that's risky.

Fantasy risks are a smorgasbord of verbal scenarios that set the stage for all kinds of intriguing possibilities. They range from risking physical danger to risking adventure and romance; from the risk of having power and control to maybe the scariest fantasy risk of all, risk being totally happy. Play out each scene in your mind's eye as best you can. Let your imagination blossom.

Say you decide to "Risk being fulfilled" and you enter into the fantasy scenario that tells you: "You have an unlimited budget to build your dream house." At last. Of course, this is a fantasy, but once invited to consider listing what you would do, you realize you already know. Somehow without much fuss you write with full gusto, laying out the whole design of a fantasy beach house or mountain lodge. You see, you have been taking creative risks all along, you just haven't dared pull them out of the nooks and crannies of your inner world and put them on paper . . . until now.

Or consider the Fantasy Risk sample. You have just won a huge amount of money from a lottery with a conscience. Imagine the exuberance as you risk trying to make the right decisions about what people and organizations deserve your funding. And when you read "List How This Event Might Affect Your Life Right Now," the sense of well-being and fulfillment from taking this short fantasy detour is vast and satisfying.

There are so many rewards from exploring fantasy risks. They massage your mind and stimulate your imagination. Imagination breeds creativity and a zest for living. So jump in and give yourself permission to whiz down a mountain, soak in a tropical ocean, or indulge in a meaningful conversation with some wise person. Fantasy risks will feed your soul and infuse your daily life with the richness and joy you truly deserve.

In five minutes you will be the next guest on Jay Leno's Tonight Show. *You will not have to perform any outlandish tricks or brag about your next movie. You just get to wear something fantastic, gab with Jay about what you think is important or funny, and share yourself with the watching world.*

List What You Would Do

_____

_____

_____

_____

_____

List Any Secret Fears

_____

_____

_____

_____

List How This Event Might Help or Affect Your Life Now

_____

_____

_____

_____

_____

*Y*ou are traveling downhill at 65 miles per hour as you crouch lower onto your racing skis high in the Alps. The chill of cool air fills your lungs as you travel faster into the white unknown. At the bottom a helicopter will meet you with your favorite hot foods, goodies, and drinks. You will then be whisked off to an elegant and remote lodge to spend two weeks skiing and enjoying the thrill of speed, challenge, and beauty.

List What You Would Do

List Any Secret Fears

List How This Event Might Help or Affect Your Life Now

You are sitting in a unique and tranquil garden of immeasurable color, fragrance, and beauty. Suddenly three people you have always admired (living, dead, or fictional) walk up to you. You have an entire day to spend talking with them about anything that comes to heart or mind.

List What You Would Do

List Any Secret Fears

List How This Event Might Help or Affect Your Life Now

*Y*ou have an unlimited budget to purchase and remodel your dream house. There is no limit to what you can create, except for your imagination. You may choose any location and size of project; all you have to do is make decisions you can live with.

List What You Would Do

_____

_____

_____

_____

_____

List Any Secret Fears

_____

_____

_____

_____

List How This Event Might Help or Affect Your Life Now

_____

_____

_____

_____

_____

*Y*ou are on a huge stage filled with sound equipment. The strap to an electric guitar is around your neck and you are playing and singing in front of 100,000 screaming rock fans. You look to your right to see your favorite rock star twirling, singing, and doing his or her thing . . . with you and the band. You stay and play through the entire set for the greatest time of your life.

List What You Would Do

List Any Secret Fears

List How This Event Might Help or Affect Your Life Now

You are standing at the edge of the open door. The wind is rushing, your heart is pounding, and then you leap into the void. Speeding downward away from the blue sky overhead, you sense a pure rush of falling. You pull the rip cord and your world seems to stop. Floating slowing downward you realize the sheer beauty and magnitude of the earth. It seems like forever until you touch down to a safe and incredible union with terra firma.

List What You Would Do

List Any Secret Fears

List How This Event Might Help or Affect Your Life Now

You find yourself sitting amid a thousand switches, dials, gauges, levers, and controls. In front of you are two windows filled with blue sky and a person sitting next to you in the cockpit of a jumbo 747 airliner. You are en route to Los Angeles, piloting more than 200 passengers. You have always dreamed about this happening . . . now it is, and you seem to know exactly what to do.

List What You Would Do

List Any Secret Fears

List How This Event Might Help or Affect Your Life Now

*Y*ou have just won $3 million dollars from the lottery. This lottery, however, is different. You cannot use the money unless you spend all of your winnings to improve the environment (plants, animals, trees, habitats) or to help other people or less fortunate nations. You have two months to do this or you lose the opportunity.

List What You Would Do

List Any Secret Fears

List How This Event Might Help or Affect Your Life Now

You are sitting in the White House. The president arrives to greet and invite you to join him and other world leaders for dinner. You have a list of complaints, suggestions, and thoughts to express in the next sixty minutes you have with him and his party.

List What You Would Do

List Any Secret Fears

List How This Event Might Help or Affect Your Life Now

You find yourself sitting in the hot shade, dusting off a small crevice of sand with a special tool. You are under the Egyptian sky exploring and participating in an archaeological dig. The potential exists to discover the missing link and make real history if you can bear the unearthly spirits all about the project. You are riveted, scared, and excited as you dig further and further.

List What You Would Do

List Any Secret Fears

List How This Event Might Help or Affect Your Life Now

---

*Y*ou own a high-fashion restaurant in New York City. It is, for the moment, very successful and unique. Your job now is to keep it that way by redesigning the menu to attract even more attention. You have access to the best international chefs, yet you must now create a mix of different palettes and spices, something that has never been done before.

List What You Would Do

_____

_____

_____

_____

List Any Secret Fears

_____

_____

_____

_____

List How This Event Might Help or Affect Your Life Now

_____

_____

_____

_____

*T*hree, two, one, the checkered flag falls and you floor it. In a split second you're smashed against the side of your formula racer. Upon reaching 180 miles per hour, you slingshot through the first turn of the Indianapolis 500. Now you are up to 225 miles per hour on the straightaway, with only 499 more laps to go. The world is a blur, and you can't hear, smell, see, or feel anything but the vibrating wheel and the track in front of you. All you have to do is hold on and go real fast for as long as you can take it.

List What You Would Do

List Any Secret Fears

List How This Event Might Help or Affect Your Life Now

You find yourself mounted on an incredible horse in a starting gate of the Kentucky Derby. You are on the favored steed to win. You duck down, tuck in, catch your breath, and remember that all you have to do is hold on and prepare for the ride of your life.

List What You Would Do

List Any Secret Fears

List How This Event Might Help or Affect Your Life Now

*Y*ou awake on a small beautiful beach of white and pink sand. The breeze is gentle as it sweeps through the palms. The water is crystal, aqua blue-green, and there is no doubt you are in paradise. You can stay here and live to be 100, or do all you can to somehow find your way back to "civilization."

List What You Would Do

List Any Secret Fears

List How This Event Might Help or Affect Your Life Now

*C*ongratulations . . . you are getting married. The wedding is in a week and you have an unlimited budget to create the party of your dreams. Fly all your friends to Bora Bora, order 10,000 delights, film the entire event, go to the moon, just use your imagination.

List What You Would Do

_____

_____

_____

_____

List Any Secret Fears

_____

_____

_____

_____

List How This Event Might Help or Affect Your Life Now

_____

_____

_____

_____

*Y*ou are preparing for travel. Only this time it's not going to be for two weeks. You are taking a year to travel the world without any restrictions. Wherever you can think of, you will go and finally have the time to absorb all there is to see, smell, and taste. Your list is long and it should prove to be the ultimate experience.

List What You Would Do

_____

_____

_____

_____

_____

List Any Secret Fears

_____

_____

_____

_____

List How This Event Might Help or Affect Your Life Now

_____

_____

_____

_____

*Y*ou are on a very large movie set filled with hustling people and equipment. You are invited to play a role in a major Hollywood picture. You discover you will be playing opposite actors such as Harrison Ford, Gwyneth Paltrow, and many of your favorite stars in their latest blockbuster. You will be surrounded with great talent and support; the rest is up to you.

List What You Would Do

_____

_____

_____

_____

List Any Secret Fears

_____

_____

_____

_____

List How This Event Might Help or Affect Your Life Now

_____

_____

_____

_____

_____

*Y*ou are floating! Soon you realize that you are floating in a spaceship high above Earth. You are on the latest space shuttle mission en route to Mars along with a few other crew members. You have been given the privilege to choose the other astronauts and the particular mission because you have something very important you always wanted to accomplish.

List What You Would Do

_____

_____

_____

_____

_____

List Any Secret Fears

_____

_____

_____

_____

List How This Event Might Help or Affect Your Life Now

_____

_____

_____

_____

*Y*ou are now in a location where you always wanted to be. Your health is perfect. In fact, you can choose to be any age and feel any way you want. You feel great—vital, absolutely happy, finally how you have always wanted to feel. One thing, you must remain there to continue this excellent state and the adventure ahead. Where are you and for how long will you stay?

List What You Would Do

List Any Secret Fears

List How This Event Might Help or Affect Your Life Now

You find yourself sitting in a beautiful and austere monastery silently meditating. The room is filled with robe-clad monks doing the same silent practice. You are now a part of their program of rituals and service. You will stay here for six months of incredible transformation.

List What You Would Do

_____

_____

_____

_____

_____

List Any Secret Fears

_____

_____

_____

_____

_____

List How This Event Might Help or Affect Your Life Now

_____

_____

_____

_____

_____

CHAPTER
FOUR
*Risk Telling
the Truth*

Risk telling the truth to your boss about . . .

"You ego-driven gas bag. How long do I have to go through this song and dance to simply get you out of the way so I can do my work! Can't you see I know exactly what to do without you looking over my shoulder and controlling everything and everyone in sight!"

List Why You Have Kept This to Yourself

Well, there just wasn't a moment for this kind of feedback. And of course I'm afraid I'll get in trouble or fired. It isn't appropriate office talk, and there's never an opportunity to really tell the truth. I've learned to keep my mouth shut.

List How Telling This Truth Might Influence Your Life Now

It might create more of a bond; once said, I might be able to laugh and detach from the anger a little. It's good not to keep things inside. I'll feel some relief and maybe a little peace. Writing it down helps clarify things a little. On paper I can read it and maybe let it go. Or maybe not. Maybe I'll say it and see what happens and feel more powerful in my work life.

RISK TELLING
the Truth

T his is the ultimate risk. Why is it so difficult? Why is it so scary? We all make compromises in telling the truth. We don't want to hurt anyone, we don't want to be too blunt, too harsh, or too honest. We learn to stretch the truth to protect others. It sounds kind, but so often it backfires and limits the depth and richness of our relationships in the workplace, with our loved ones, and most important, with ourselves. Risking the truth is really about facing who we really are, embracing both our strengths and our weaknesses. No excuses, or hidden agenda.

Risk Telling the Truth is divided into two parts. Part One is about telling the truth to others about the things that really irk you. It's time to finally get it off your chest. For example, "Risk telling the truth to your boss." Wow! Is that even legal? It could change the entire dynamic of your workplace, and yes it might make a mess at first. Of course, this risk is still on paper . . . so give it your best shot. As you rant and rave and give voice to the hidden, less polite you, notice how much better you feel.

In the Risk Telling the Truth sample you'll read a whole litany of fear-laden excuses and really good reasons about not telling it like it is. And in the answers to "List Why You Have Kept This to Yourself" you may come to realize that not telling the truth can create a pretty big problem in terms of plain old self-respect and personal integrity. Forget about your job—how about your relationship with yourself? Whether you choose to really tell your boss what's on your mind is up to you. It may not be the appropriate time or place . . . yet. But writing it down will open up a whole new perspective and might even give you a chance to pause, reassess, and laugh a little.

Part Two in Risk Telling the Truth cuts to the chase. It's a real showdown between you and you, as in "Risk telling the truth to yourself about . . . " and covers subjects from appearance to habits you'd like to quit to skeletons in your closet. Being honest, even if it's only on paper, can change your life forever for the better. Consider "Risk telling yourself the truth about your finances." Try it, no holds barred. The result of your soul searching will bring you endless rewards.

Risk Telling the Truth builds character and enhances integrity. Whether you dare to take your discoveries into the world or keep them private is your choice. No matter, you'll have proven you have the courage to take the risk. Guaranteed, if you get through a few of these, you'll be able to look yourself in the mirror and truly like who you see.

PART ONE:
Risk Telling the Truth to Others

Risk telling the truth to your boss about . . .

List Why You Have Kept This to Yourself

List How Telling This Truth Might Influence Your Life Now

Risk telling the truth to your therapist about . . .

_____

_____

_____

_____

_____

_____

_____

List Why You Have Kept This to Yourself

_____

_____

_____

_____

List How Telling This Truth Might Influence Your Life Now

_____

_____

_____

_____

Risk telling the truth to your doctor about . . .

_____

_____

_____

_____

_____

_____

_____

_____

List Why You Have Kept This to Yourself

_____

_____

_____

_____

List How Telling This Truth Might Influence Your Life Now

_____

_____

_____

_____

_____

Risk telling the truth to the IRS about . . .

_____

_____

_____

_____

_____

_____

_____

List Why You Have Kept This to Yourself

_____

_____

_____

_____

List How Telling This Truth Might Influence Your Life Now

_____

_____

_____

_____

Risk telling the truth to your rabbi/priest about . . .

_____

_____

_____

_____

_____

_____

_____

_____

List Why You Have Kept This to Yourself

_____

_____

_____

_____

List How Telling This Truth Might Influence Your Life Now

_____

_____

_____

_____

_____

Risk telling the truth to your landlord about . . .

_____

_____

_____

_____

_____

_____

List Why You Have Kept This to Yourself

_____

_____

_____

_____

List How Telling This Truth Might Influence Your Life Now

_____

_____

_____

_____

_____

Risk telling the truth to your significant other about . . .

_____

_____

_____

_____

_____

_____

_____

List Why You Have Kept This to Yourself

_____

_____

_____

_____

List How Telling This Truth Might Influence Your Life Now

_____

_____

_____

_____

_____

Risk telling the truth to your business partner about ...

_____

_____

_____

_____

_____

_____

List Why You Have Kept This to Yourself

_____

_____

_____

_____

List How Telling This Truth Might Influence Your Life Now

_____

_____

_____

_____

_____

Risk telling the truth to your children about . . .

_____

_____

_____

_____

_____

_____

_____

List Why You Have Kept This to Yourself

_____

_____

_____

_____

List How Telling This Truth Might Influence Your Life Now

_____

_____

_____

_____

Risk telling the truth to your wife/husband about . . .

_____

_____

_____

_____

_____

_____

List Why You Have Kept This to Yourself

_____

_____

_____

_____

List How Telling This Truth Might Influence Your Life Now

_____

_____

_____

_____

Risk telling the truth to your lover about . . .

_____
_____
_____
_____
_____
_____
_____
_____

List Why You Have Kept This to Yourself

_____
_____
_____
_____

List How Telling This Truth Might Influence Your Life Now

_____
_____
_____
_____
_____

Risk telling the truth to your mother about . . .

_____

_____

_____

_____

_____

_____

List Why You Have Kept This to Yourself

_____

_____

_____

_____

List How Telling This Truth Might Influence Your Life Now

_____

_____

_____

_____

_____

Risk telling the truth to your father about . . .

_____

_____

_____

_____

_____

_____

_____

_____

List Why You Have Kept This to Yourself

_____

_____

_____

_____

List How Telling This Truth Might Influence Your Life Now

_____

_____

_____

_____

Risk telling the truth to your sister about . . .

_____

_____

_____

_____

_____

_____

_____

List Why You Have Kept This to Yourself

_____

_____

_____

_____

List How Telling This Truth Might Influence Your Life Now

_____

_____

_____

_____

Risk telling the truth to your brother about . . .

_____

_____

_____

_____

_____

_____

_____

_____

List Why You Have Kept This to Yourself

_____

_____

_____

_____

List How Telling This Truth Might Influence Your Life Now

_____

_____

_____

_____

Risk telling the truth to your best friend about . . .

_____

_____

_____

_____

_____

_____

_____

List Why You Have Kept This to Yourself

_____

_____

_____

_____

List How Telling This Truth Might Influence Your Life Now

_____

_____

_____

_____

Risk telling the truth to your in-laws about . . .

_____

_____

_____

_____

_____

_____

_____

_____

_____

List Why You Have Kept This to Yourself

_____

_____

_____

_____

List How Telling This Truth Might Influence Your Life Now

_____

_____

_____

_____

_____

Risk telling the truth to your coworkers about . . .

_____

_____

_____

_____

_____

_____

_____

_____

List Why You Have Kept This to Yourself

_____

_____

_____

_____

List How Telling This Truth Might Influence Your Life Now

_____

_____

_____

_____

Risk telling the truth to your neighbors about . . .

_____

_____

_____

_____

_____

_____

_____

_____

_____

List Why You Have Kept This to Yourself

_____

_____

_____

_____

List How Telling This Truth Might Influence Your Life Now

_____

_____

_____

_____

_____

Risk telling the truth to your roommate about . . .

_____

_____

_____

_____

_____

_____

_____

List Why You Have Kept This to Yourself

_____

_____

_____

_____

List How Telling This Truth Might Influence Your Life Now

_____

_____

_____

_____

Risk telling the truth to your teacher about . . .

_____

_____

_____

_____

_____

_____

_____

_____

List Why You Have Kept This to Yourself

_____

_____

_____

_____

List How Telling This Truth Might Influence Your Life Now

_____

_____

_____

_____

Risk telling the truth to a stranger about . . .

_____

_____

_____

_____

_____

_____

_____

List Why You Have Kept This to Yourself

_____

_____

_____

_____

List How Telling This Truth Might Influence Your Life Now

_____

_____

_____

_____

_____

Risk telling the truth to your baby-sitter about . . .

List Why You Have Kept This to Yourself

List How Telling This Truth Might Influence Your Life Now

Risk telling the truth to a collection agency about . . .

_____

_____

_____

_____

_____

_____

_____

_____

List Why You Have Kept This to Yourself

_____

_____

_____

_____

_____

List How Telling This Truth Might Influence Your Life Now

_____

_____

_____

_____

_____

Risk telling the truth to a telemarketer about . . .

_____

_____

_____

_____

_____

_____

_____

_____

List Why You Have Kept This to Yourself

_____

_____

_____

_____

List How Telling This Truth Might Influence Your Life Now

_____

_____

_____

_____

PART TWO:
Risk Telling the Truth to Yourself

Risk telling the truth to yourself about your finances.

_____

_____

_____

_____

_____

_____

_____

_____

List Why You Have Kept This to Yourself

_____

_____

_____

_____

List How Telling This Truth Might Influence Your Life Now

_____

_____

_____

_____

_____

Risk telling the truth to
yourself about your credit rating.

_____

_____

_____

_____

_____

_____

List Why You Have Kept This to Yourself

_____

_____

_____

_____

List How Telling This Truth Might Influence Your Life Now

_____

_____

_____

_____

Risk telling the truth to
yourself about your education.

_____
_____
_____
_____
_____
_____
_____

List Why You Have Kept This to Yourself

_____
_____
_____
_____

List How Telling This Truth Might Influence Your Life Now

_____
_____
_____
_____
_____

Risk telling the truth to
yourself about your medical history.

_____

_____

_____

_____

_____

_____

List Why You Have Kept This to Yourself

_____

_____

_____

_____

_____

List How Telling This Truth Might Influence Your Life Now

_____

_____

_____

_____

_____

Risk telling the truth to
yourself about your health.

_____

_____

_____

_____

_____

_____

_____

List Why You Have Kept This to Yourself

_____

_____

_____

_____

List How Telling This Truth Might Influence Your Life Now

_____

_____

_____

_____

_____

Risk telling the truth to
yourself about your feelings today.

_____

_____

_____

_____

_____

_____

List Why You Have Kept This to Yourself

_____

_____

_____

_____

List How Telling This Truth Might Influence Your Life Now

_____

_____

_____

_____

_____

Risk telling the truth to yourself about your childhood.

_____

_____

_____

_____

_____

_____

List Why You Have Kept This to Yourself

_____

_____

_____

_____

List How Telling This Truth Might Influence Your Life Now

_____

_____

_____

_____

Risk telling the truth to yourself about the skeletons in your closet.

_____

_____

_____

_____

_____

_____

List Why You Have Kept This to Yourself

_____

_____

_____

_____

List How Telling This Truth Might Influence Your Life Now

_____

_____

_____

_____

Risk telling the truth to
yourself about your work.

List Why You Have Kept This to Yourself

List How Telling This Truth Might Influence Your Life Now

Risk telling the truth to yourself about your dreams.

_____

_____

_____

_____

_____

_____

List Why You Have Kept This to Yourself

_____

_____

_____

_____

List How Telling This Truth Might Influence Your Life Now

_____

_____

_____

_____

Risk telling the truth to yourself about your worst habits.

_____

_____

_____

_____

_____

_____

_____

List Why You Have Kept This to Yourself

_____

_____

_____

_____

_____

List How Telling This Truth Might Influence Your Life Now

_____

_____

_____

_____

_____

Risk telling the truth
to yourself about your past.

_____

_____

_____

_____

_____

_____

List Why You Have Kept This to Yourself

_____

_____

_____

_____

_____

List How Telling This Truth Might Influence Your Life Now

_____

_____

_____

_____

_____

Risk telling the truth to yourself about your sex life.

_____

_____

_____

_____

_____

_____

_____

_____

List Why You Have Kept This to Yourself

_____

_____

_____

_____

_____

List How Telling This Truth Might Influence Your Life Now

_____

_____

_____

_____

_____

Risk telling the truth to yourself about your physical appearance.

_____

_____

_____

_____

_____

_____

_____

List Why You Have Kept This to Yourself

_____

_____

_____

_____

_____

List How Telling This Truth Might Influence Your Life Now

_____

_____

_____

_____

_____

Risk telling the truth to yourself about your political position.

_____

_____

_____

_____

_____

_____

_____

List Why You Have Kept This to Yourself

_____

_____

_____

_____

_____

List How Telling This Truth Might Influence Your Life Now

_____

_____

_____

_____

_____

Risk telling the truth to yourself about your secret passions.

_____

_____

_____

_____

_____

_____

_____

List Why You Have Kept This to Yourself

_____

_____

_____

_____

List How Telling This Truth Might Influence Your Life Now

_____

_____

_____

_____

Risk telling the truth to
yourself about your family.

_____

_____

_____

_____

_____

_____

List Why You Have Kept This to Yourself

_____

_____

_____

_____

List How Telling This Truth Might Influence Your Life Now

_____

_____

_____

_____

Risk telling the truth to
yourself about your relationships.

_____

_____

_____

_____

_____

_____

List Why You Have Kept This to Yourself

_____

_____

_____

_____

List How Telling This Truth Might Influence Your Life Now

_____

_____

_____

_____

_____

Risk telling the truth to
yourself about your eating habits.

_____

_____

_____

_____

_____

_____

_____

List Why You Have Kept This to Yourself

_____

_____

_____

_____

List How Telling This Truth Might Influence Your Life Now

_____

_____

_____

_____

Risk telling the truth to
yourself about your worst fears.

_____

_____

_____

_____

_____

_____

List Why You Have Kept This to Yourself

_____

_____

_____

_____

List How Telling This Truth Might Influence Your Life Now

_____

_____

_____

_____

Risk telling the truth to
yourself about your pet peeves.

List Why You Have Kept This to Yourself

List How Telling This Truth Might Influence Your Life Now

Risk telling the truth
to yourself about your age.

_____

_____

_____

_____

_____

_____

List Why You Have Kept This to Yourself

_____

_____

_____

_____

List How Telling This Truth Might Influence Your Life Now

_____

_____

_____

_____

_____

Risk telling the truth to yourself about your transgressions.

_____

_____

_____

_____

_____

_____

List Why You Have Kept This to Yourself

_____

_____

_____

_____

List How Telling This Truth Might Influence Your Life Now

_____

_____

_____

_____

_____

Risk telling the truth to yourself about your close calls with danger.

_____

_____

_____

_____

_____

_____

List Why You Have Kept This to Yourself

_____

_____

_____

_____

List How Telling This Truth Might Influence Your Life Now

_____

_____

_____

_____

_____

Risk telling the truth to yourself about your drug use.

_____

_____

_____

_____

_____

_____

_____

List Why You Have Kept This to Yourself

_____

_____

_____

_____

List How Telling This Truth Might Influence Your Life Now

_____

_____

_____

_____

Risk telling the truth to yourself about what you really do with your money.

_____

_____

_____

_____

_____

_____

List Why You Have Kept This to Yourself

_____

_____

_____

_____

List How Telling This Truth Might Influence Your Life Now

_____

_____

_____

_____

CHAPTER
FIVE
Personal Risks

Personal Risk: Risk leaving a relationship that no longer works.

List the Risks

I'll be alone and scared.

I'm so used to being a couple, I'll flip out.

I don't want to admit it failed.

I may be wrong about this.

I'll have to do everything on my own,

again

List the Worst Scenario

I'll never find anyone else, ever.

I'll be so depressed.

I'll see him or her happy with someone.

I'll die alone in the gutter.

I'll realize I made a terrible mistake.

I'll miss the really sweet times we

had and never have them again

List the Rewards

I'll meet someone better soon.

I'll find I like being alone a lot more

than I thought.

I'll have more time to do the things

I love.

My life will be elegantly simple.

I'll be in total control at last.

No more bullshit, snoring, whining, alcohol,

accusations…

List What You Are Willing to Do

Maybe we'll go see a therapist.

Maybe we'll take a short vacation

Go out with my friends and check out

the social scene.

Learn to see the good stuff and be

grateful.

Take three months and explore

possibilities before making a decision

PERSONAL *Risks*

Personal Risks is really where it's at. Now that you've gotten fluent in risk taking this is where you can customize the risk sheets to reflect the unique aspects of your life. Each page is the same as the ones you've used in the Real Risks chapter, but there is a blank for you to fill in with today's risk challenge.

Personal Risks offer you a safe place to drop in to find out more about how you think and feel, as well as what you need to do about something that is challenging you right now. From a career move to a relationship issue, from big decisions to small, simply write in today's risk and find out what's important.

For example, last night you had a difficult time with a coworker. You went to Risk Telling the Truth and filled out "Risk telling the truth to Jackie" and discovered you had some old unresolved bad feelings about her, stuff that has really impacted your job in a negative way. You realize you need to "Risk asking your supervisor to move you to another floor." You enter that risk in your Personal Risks sheet and within minutes find you are right and want to make the move. The items under "List the Rewards" are just too convincing and tomorrow you ask and receive permission to do so. From paper to Floor 25, with a better desk and a better view!

The Personal Risk sample has been filled in to illustrate the pros and cons of leaving a long-term relationship. "List the Risks . . . " and "List the Worst Scenario" give you plenty of room to unload those sticky fears that cling to us even when we know better. "I'll flip out," "I don't want to admit it failed," and "I'll never find any-one else" are legitimate, important admissions that might not sound so pretty but once said, give room for more positive hopes and realistic options. In "What Am I Willing to Do?" the list offers five actual doable scenarios, a pretty good grab bag in times of great indecision and confusion. The point is, working the risk helps. It points you in the right direction, it supports your choices, and most important, it gives you a place to consider before you act.

Personal Risks is also the right place to delve into your dreams about who you want to be. Resurrect a past plan for your life, a vision you've not been able to real-ize. Maybe you've wanted to "Risk living in southern France" for a year and just haven't dared consider the pros and cons. Try it out and see for yourself. Whatever the risk, Personal Risks is the place to write it out and risk it first on paper and then in the world. You deserve it.

Personal Risk:

List the Risks

List the Worst Scenario

List the Rewards

List What You Are Willing to Do

Personal Risk:

List the Risks

List the Worst Scenario

List the Rewards

List What You Are Willing to Do

Personal Risk:

List the Risks

List the Worst Scenario

List the Rewards

List What You Are Willing to Do

Personal Risk:

List the Risks

List the Worst Scenario

List the Rewards

List What You Are Willing to Do

Personal Risk:

List the Risks

List the Worst Scenario

List the Rewards

List What You Are Willing to Do

Personal Risk:

List the Risks

List the Worst Scenario

List the Rewards

List What You Are Willing to Do

Personal Risk:

List the Risks

List the Worst Scenario

List the Rewards

List What You Are Willing to Do

Personal Risk:

List the Risks	List the Worst Scenario

List the Rewards	List What You Are Willing to Do

Personal Risk:

List the Risks

List the Worst Scenario

List the Rewards

List What You Are Willing to Do

Personal Risk:

List the Risks

List the Worst Scenario

List the Rewards

List What You Are Willing to Do

Personal Risk:

List the Risks

List the Worst Scenario

List the Rewards

List What You Are Willing to Do

Personal Risk:

List the Risks

List the Worst Scenario

List the Rewards

List What You Are Willing to Do

Personal Risk:

List the Risks

List the Worst Scenario

List the Rewards

List What You Are Willing to Do

Personal Risk:

List the Risks

List the Worst Scenario

List the Rewards

List What You Are Willing to Do

Personal Risk:

List the Risks

List the Worst Scenario

List the Rewards

List What You Are Willing to Do

Personal Risk:

PERSONAL RISKS

List the Risks

List the Worst Scenario

List the Rewards

List What You Are Willing to Do

Personal Risk:

List the Risks

List the Worst Scenario

List the Rewards

List What You Are Willing to Do

Personal Risk:

List the Risks

List the Worst Scenario

List the Rewards

List What You Are Willing to Do

Personal Risk:

List the Risks

List the Worst Scenario

List the Rewards

List What You Are Willing to Do

Personal Risk: _____

List the Risks

List the Worst Scenario

List the Rewards

List What You Are Willing to Do

Personal Risk:

List the Risks

List the Worst Scenario

List the Rewards

List What You Are Willing to Do

Personal Risk:

List the Risks

List the Worst Scenario

List the Rewards

List What You Are Willing to Do

Personal Risk:

List the Risks

List the Worst Scenario

List the Rewards

List What You Are Willing to Do

Personal Risk:

List the Risks

List the Worst Scenario

List the Rewards

List What You Are Willing to Do

Personal Risk:

List the Risks

List the Worst Scenario

List the Rewards

List What You Are Willing to Do

Personal Risk:

List the Risks

List the Worst Scenario

List the Rewards

List What You Are Willing to Do

Personal Risk:

List the Risks

List the Worst Scenario

List the Rewards

List What You Are Willing to Do

Personal Risk:

List the Risks

List the Worst Scenario

List the Rewards

List What You Are Willing to Do

Personal Risk:

List the Risks

List the Worst Scenario

List the Rewards

List What You Are Willing to Do

Personal Risk:

PERSONAL RISKS

List the Risks

List the Worst Scenario

List the Rewards

List What You Are Willing to Do